W9-CJZ-182

Graham Meadows & Claire Vial

Contents

Dominie Press, Inc.

About Hippos

Hippo is another word for *hippopotamus*. Hippos live in Africa. There are two kinds of hippos—the pygmy hippo and the common hippo. This book is about common hippos. They can be found in many parts of Africa. They live in open areas where there is enough water to drink and plants to eat.

The ancient Greeks called hippos "river horses." The Greek word for *horse* is *hippo*.

Swahili is a language that is spoken in many parts of East Africa. The Swahili word for *hippopotamus* is *kiboko*.

Where They Live

When you see a common hippo in the water, usually all you can see is its head. But hidden beneath the water's surface is the body of one of the largest land animals in the world.

Hippos prefer lakes or slow-moving rivers where they can stand on the bottom, and where the water is just deep enough to cover their bodies. A hippo can rest in the water for long periods of time because its **nostrils**, eyes, and ears are located high on its huge head.

Adult hippos can hold their breath for up to six minutes while they are under water.

Where They Live

Hippos are more at home in water than on land. The water keeps them cool. It also helps to keep their sensitive skin moist and protect it from the hot sun.

Hippos spend up to ten hours a day resting or swimming in water. They also enjoy taking mud baths. They lie along river banks in muddy areas called wallows. The mud protects their skin from the hot sun and biting insects.

Birds such as cattle egrets often perch on hippos and eat some of the biting insects on their skin.

Their Bodies

Hippos have huge heads. Their large bodies are shaped like barrels, and they have short, strong legs. Adult males can grow to be up to five feet tall and eleven feet long. They can weigh up to 7,000 pounds. Females are smaller than males and can weigh up to 5,000 pounds.

A hippo's smooth skin is mostly gray-brown in color. The only hairs on its body are short **bristles** on its **muzzle**, ears, and tail. Its tail is short and shaped like a paddle with flat sides.

A hippo's head can be up to one-third of its total body length.

Their Bodies

When it is resting in the water, a hippo can stay almost completely under the surface but still see, breathe, and smell. This allows the hippo to stay alert to **predators**, such as crocodiles and humans. Some humans hunt hippos for food or for their hides.

When a hippo dives under water, it uses special muscles to close its nostrils and ears. These special muscles keep out the water. When the hippo returns to the surface, it snorts to clear water away from its nostrils. At the same time, it moves its ears to shake away any water.

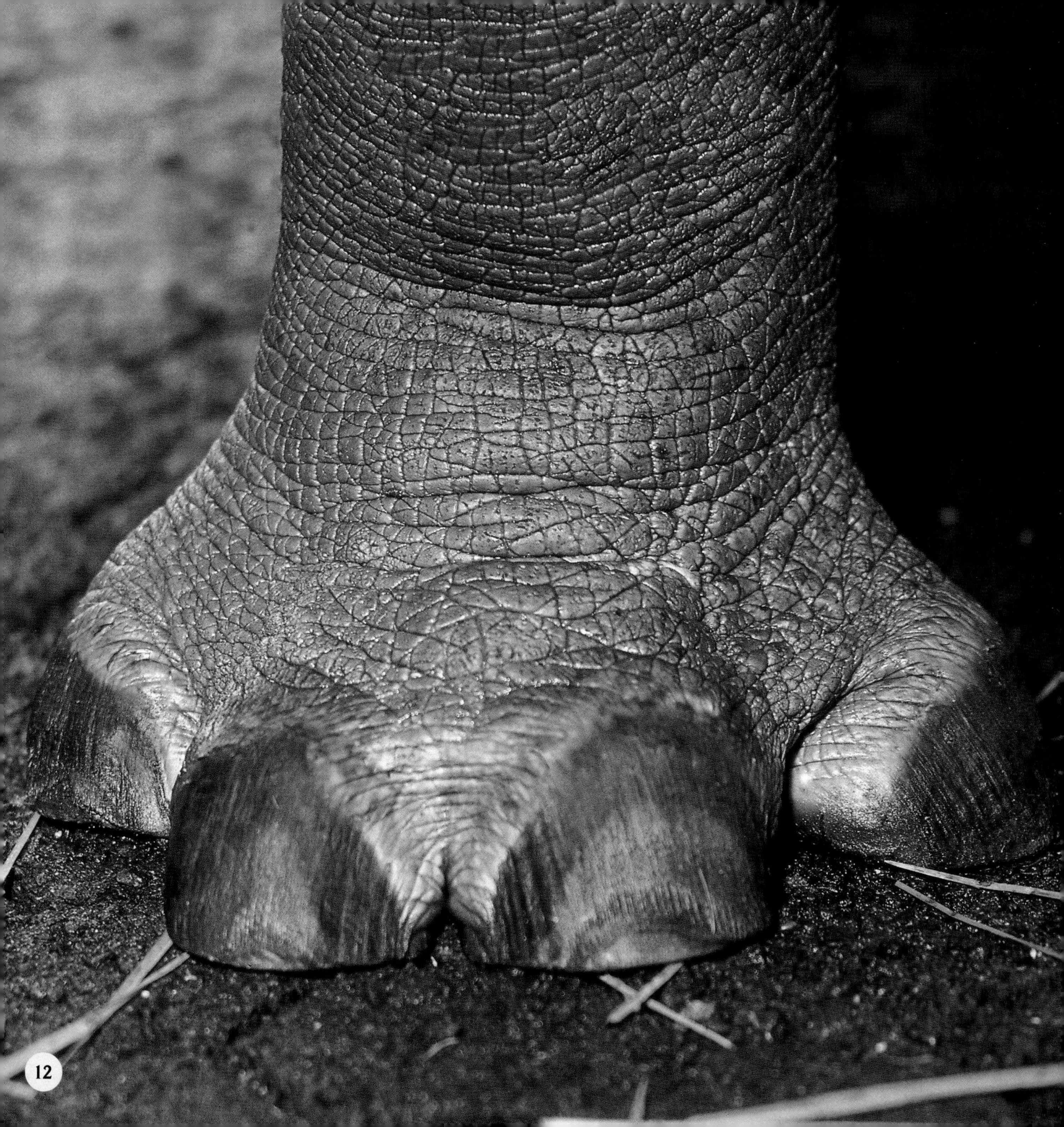

Their Bodies

Hippos have four toes on each foot. The toes are connected by small flaps of skin, like the web on a duck's feet. The toe flaps help hippos to swim.

When they move around in the water, hippos use their hind legs to push themselves off the bottom of a river or a lake. Then they tuck their legs close to their bodies and glide through the water until they sink to the bottom again. Their front legs touch the bottom first, and then they push themselves again with their hind legs.

When a hippo swims, it uses its tail to steer.

Their Diet

Hippos are **herbivores**, which means they eat only plants. They eat plants in the water during the day, and come out of the water at night to feed on land plants. An hour or two before sunset, they start to walk to their feeding areas.

As they walk along, they use their wide lips to tear off mouthfuls of green grass. They **graze** for about five hours each night. During that time, they can eat more than 250 pounds of grass and travel up to six miles.

Hippos can trot along at about ten miles an hour, but they can **gallop** at up to thirty miles an hour for a short distance if they need to.

Their Teeth

Hippos have forty teeth. Their back teeth are called **molars**. They use them to crush and grind the plants they eat.

Hippos have a pair of sharp front teeth called **incisors** on their upper and lower jaws. Next to the incisors are their canine teeth, or tusks. The canine teeth can grow as long as twenty inches. They are used for attack and defense.

When a hippo yawns, it isn't because it is tired. A hippo uses a yawn to threaten other animals or to challenge them to a fight.

Their Families

Hippos spend the day in groups called **herds**, or schools. The size of these herds varies. Some groups contain just five animals, while others are made up of more than 100 hippos. Some herds contain both males and females. Others, called bachelor herds, are made up entirely of males.

Male hippos are called bulls. Females are called cows. Young hippos are called calves.

Cows and calves sometimes come together to form a nursery school, or créche. This helps to keep the calves safe from predators.

When They Mate

Male hippos usually **mate** when they are about five years old. Females mate when they are about seven years old. A female hippo usually has one calf every two years.

Hippos usually mate during the dry season, when little or no rain falls and the grass does not grow very much. Their calves are born eight months later, during the rainy season. This is when the grass is starting to grow again and there is plenty of food.

Their Young

When a female hippo is due to give birth, she leaves the herd. She does not return until after the calf is born.

Most hippo calves are born under water. **Instinct** tells them how to reach the surface to get their first breath. Calves weigh between 50 and 120 pounds at birth and are about three feet long. They can **suckle**, or drink their mothers' milk, under water as well as on land. They are **weaned** by the time they are about eight months old.

Hippos can live as long as thirty-five years in the **wild**. These huge "river horses" are among the most interesting animals in the world.

Glossary

bristles: Thick, stiff hairs
gallop: To run very fast
graze: To eat, or feed on plants
herbivores: Animals that eat plants
herds: Groups of animals that have a common bond and live together like a family
incisors: Teeth used for cutting
instinct: A natural feeling
mate: To join with another animal in order to produce offspring
molars: Teeth with rounded or flattened surfaces used for grinding
muzzle: An animal's mouth and nose
nostrils: Part of the nose
predators: Animals that hunt and kill other animals
suckle: To drink a mother's milk
Swahili: A language that is spoken in many parts of East Africa
weaned: No longer drinking a mother's milk; able to find and eat other food
wild: Natural surroundings; not a zoo

Index

Publisher: Raymond Yuen
Editor: Bob Rowland
Designer: Carol Anne Craft

Published by:

Dominie Press, Inc.

1949 Kellogg Avenue
Carlsbad, California 92008 USA

ISBN 0-7685-0964-5

Printed in Singapore by PH Productions Pte Ltd
1 2 3 4 5 6 PH 02 01 00

www.dominie.com